50 Frozen Bliss Recipes for Home

By: Kelly Johnson

Table of Contents

- Classic Vanilla Ice Cream
- Chocolate Fudge Brownie Sundae
- Strawberry Cheesecake Sorbet
- Mango Coconut Gelato
- Mint Chocolate Chip Ice Cream
- Raspberry Lemonade Granita
- Salted Caramel Swirl Frozen Yogurt
- Blueberry Basil Sorbet
- Peanut Butter Cup Ice Cream
- Pina Colada Sorbet
- Matcha Green Tea Ice Cream
- Cookies and Cream Gelato
- Peach Melba Granita
- Mocha Almond Fudge Ice Cream
- Pineapple Coconut Frozen Smoothie
- Raspberry White Chocolate Gelato
- Lemon Basil Sorbet
- Hazelnut Coffee Ice Cream
- Blackberry Mint Frozen Yogurt
- Cinnamon Roll Ice Cream
- Watermelon Mint Granita
- Pumpkin Spice Frozen Custard
- Chocolate Raspberry Sorbet
- Almond Joy Gelato
- Key Lime Pie Frozen Yogurt
- Espresso Affogato
- Cherry Vanilla Ice Cream
- Tropical Fruit Sorbet
- Nutella Swirl Gelato
- Spiced Apple Frozen Smoothie
- Hibiscus Raspberry Sorbet
- Caramel Macchiato Ice Cream
- Lemon Blueberry Cheesecake Gelato
- White Chocolate Ginger Frozen Yogurt
- Classic Strawberry Ice Cream
- Mango Passionfruit Sorbet

- Tiramisu Gelato
- Fig and Honey Ice Cream
- Matcha Red Bean Sorbet
- S'mores Frozen Custard
- Pineapple Mint Gelato
- Chai Tea Ice Cream
- Pear Vanilla Sorbet
- Dark Chocolate Chili Ice Cream
- Coconut Lychee Gelato
- Blackberry Lemonade Granita
- Brownie Batter Frozen Yogurt
- Pomegranate Citrus Sorbet
- Spumoni Ice Cream
- Banana Cream Pie Gelato

Classic Vanilla Ice Cream

Ingredients:

- 2 cups heavy cream
- 1 cup whole milk
- 3/4 cup granulated sugar
- 1 tablespoon pure vanilla extract
- Pinch of salt

Instructions:

1. **Combine Ingredients**: In a medium bowl, whisk together the granulated sugar and salt with the whole milk until the sugar is fully dissolved. Stir in the heavy cream and vanilla extract.
2. **Chill Mixture**: Cover the bowl with plastic wrap and refrigerate the mixture for at least 1 hour, or until it is thoroughly chilled.
3. **Churn Ice Cream**: Pour the chilled mixture into an ice cream maker and churn according to the manufacturer's instructions. This typically takes about 20-25 minutes, or until the ice cream reaches a soft-serve consistency.
4. **Freeze**: Transfer the churned ice cream to an airtight container. Freeze for at least 2 hours, or until it reaches a firm consistency.
5. **Serve**: Scoop and enjoy your classic vanilla ice cream!

Chocolate Fudge Brownie Sundae

Ingredients:

For the Brownies:

- 1/2 cup (1 stick) unsalted butter
- 1 cup granulated sugar
- 2 large eggs
- 1 teaspoon vanilla extract
- 1/3 cup unsweetened cocoa powder
- 1/2 cup all-purpose flour
- 1/4 teaspoon salt
- 1/4 teaspoon baking powder

For the Sundae:

- Vanilla ice cream (store-bought or homemade)
- 1 cup chocolate fudge sauce (store-bought or homemade)
- Whipped cream
- Maraschino cherries
- Crushed nuts (optional)

Instructions:

1. **Prepare Brownies**: Preheat your oven to 350°F (175°C). Grease and flour an 8x8-inch baking pan. In a medium saucepan, melt the butter over low heat. Remove from heat and stir in sugar, eggs, and vanilla extract. Beat in cocoa powder, flour, salt, and baking powder until well combined. Pour the batter into the prepared pan.
2. **Bake Brownies**: Bake for 20-25 minutes, or until a toothpick inserted into the center comes out with a few moist crumbs. Let the brownies cool completely in the pan on a wire rack. Once cooled, cut into squares.
3. **Assemble Sundaes**: Place a brownie square in a serving dish or bowl. Top with a scoop of vanilla ice cream. Drizzle generously with chocolate fudge sauce. Add a dollop of whipped cream on top.
4. **Garnish**: Finish with a maraschino cherry and a sprinkle of crushed nuts, if desired.
5. **Serve**: Enjoy your decadent Chocolate Fudge Brownie Sundae immediately!

Strawberry Cheesecake Sorbet

Ingredients:

- 2 cups fresh strawberries, hulled and halved
- 1 cup granulated sugar
- 1 cup water
- 1 tablespoon lemon juice
- 1/2 cup cream cheese, softened
- 1 teaspoon vanilla extract

Instructions:

1. **Prepare Strawberry Mixture**: In a blender or food processor, combine the fresh strawberries and granulated sugar. Blend until smooth.
2. **Make Syrup**: In a small saucepan, heat the water over medium heat until it begins to simmer. Stir in the remaining sugar until dissolved completely. Allow the syrup to cool to room temperature.
3. **Combine Ingredients**: Once the syrup has cooled, add it to the blended strawberry mixture. Stir in the lemon juice, vanilla extract, and softened cream cheese until smooth and well combined.
4. **Chill Mixture**: Refrigerate the mixture for at least 1 hour to ensure it is thoroughly chilled.
5. **Churn Sorbet**: Pour the chilled mixture into an ice cream maker and churn according to the manufacturer's instructions. This usually takes about 20-25 minutes, or until the sorbet reaches a soft-serve consistency.
6. **Freeze**: Transfer the churned sorbet to an airtight container. Freeze for at least 2 hours, or until it is firm.
7. **Serve**: Scoop and enjoy your refreshing Strawberry Cheesecake Sorbet!

Mango Coconut Gelato

Ingredients:

- 2 cups ripe mango, peeled and diced
- 1 cup coconut milk
- 1 cup heavy cream
- 3/4 cup granulated sugar
- 1/4 cup honey or agave syrup
- 1 teaspoon vanilla extract
- 1/4 teaspoon salt

Instructions:

1. **Prepare Mango Puree**: In a blender or food processor, combine the diced mango and half of the granulated sugar. Blend until smooth. Set aside.
2. **Heat Dairy**: In a medium saucepan, combine the coconut milk, heavy cream, and the remaining granulated sugar. Heat over medium heat until the sugar is fully dissolved and the mixture is warmed, but not boiling. Remove from heat and stir in the honey (or agave syrup), vanilla extract, and salt.
3. **Combine Mixtures**: Stir the mango puree into the warm coconut cream mixture until fully combined.
4. **Chill Mixture**: Refrigerate the mixture for at least 1 hour, or until it is thoroughly chilled.
5. **Churn Gelato**: Pour the chilled mixture into an ice cream maker and churn according to the manufacturer's instructions. This typically takes about 20-25 minutes, or until the gelato reaches a smooth, creamy texture.
6. **Freeze**: Transfer the churned gelato to an airtight container. Freeze for at least 2 hours, or until it is firm.
7. **Serve**: Scoop and enjoy your creamy Mango Coconut Gelato!

Mint Chocolate Chip Ice Cream

Ingredients:

- 2 cups heavy cream
- 1 cup whole milk
- 3/4 cup granulated sugar
- 1 teaspoon pure vanilla extract
- 1 teaspoon pure peppermint extract
- 1/2 cup mini chocolate chips
- A few drops of green food coloring (optional)

Instructions:

1. **Combine Ingredients**: In a medium bowl, whisk together the granulated sugar and whole milk until the sugar is fully dissolved. Stir in the heavy cream, vanilla extract, and peppermint extract. If using, add a few drops of green food coloring to achieve the desired minty color.
2. **Chill Mixture**: Cover the bowl with plastic wrap and refrigerate for at least 1 hour, or until the mixture is thoroughly chilled.
3. **Churn Ice Cream**: Pour the chilled mixture into an ice cream maker and churn according to the manufacturer's instructions. This usually takes about 20-25 minutes, or until the ice cream reaches a soft-serve consistency.
4. **Add Chocolate Chips**: During the last 5 minutes of churning, add the mini chocolate chips to the ice cream maker.
5. **Freeze**: Transfer the churned ice cream to an airtight container. Freeze for at least 2 hours, or until it reaches a firm consistency.
6. **Serve**: Scoop and enjoy your refreshing Mint Chocolate Chip Ice Cream

Raspberry Lemonade Granita

Ingredients:

- 2 cups fresh raspberries
- 1 cup freshly squeezed lemon juice (about 4 lemons)
- 3/4 cup granulated sugar
- 1 cup water
- 1 teaspoon lemon zest (optional)

Instructions:

1. **Prepare Raspberry Puree**: In a blender or food processor, combine the fresh raspberries and 1/4 cup of the granulated sugar. Blend until smooth. Strain the mixture through a fine-mesh sieve to remove the seeds, pressing with a spatula to extract as much juice as possible.
2. **Make Lemonade Base**: In a medium bowl, whisk together the remaining granulated sugar and water until the sugar is completely dissolved. Stir in the freshly squeezed lemon juice and lemon zest (if using).
3. **Combine Mixtures**: Add the raspberry puree to the lemon juice mixture and stir until well combined.
4. **Freeze Mixture**: Pour the mixture into a shallow baking dish. Place in the freezer.
5. **Scrape Granita**: After 30 minutes, use a fork to scrape and stir the granita, breaking up any ice crystals that have formed. Continue to scrape and stir every 30 minutes until the granita is fully frozen and has a fluffy, snow-like texture. This usually takes about 2-3 hours.
6. **Serve**: Scoop the granita into glasses or bowls and serve immediately. Enjoy the refreshing and tangy Raspberry Lemonade Granita!

Salted Caramel Swirl Frozen Yogurt

Ingredients:

For the Frozen Yogurt:

- 2 cups plain Greek yogurt (full-fat or 2%)
- 1 cup heavy cream
- 3/4 cup granulated sugar
- 1 teaspoon vanilla extract
- 1/2 teaspoon sea salt

For the Salted Caramel Sauce:

- 1 cup granulated sugar
- 6 tablespoons unsalted butter
- 1/2 cup heavy cream
- 1/2 teaspoon sea salt

Instructions:

1. **Make Salted Caramel Sauce**:
    1. In a medium saucepan over medium heat, melt the granulated sugar, stirring constantly until it turns a deep amber color.
    2. Carefully add the butter and stir until melted and combined. The mixture will bubble vigorously.
    3. Slowly add the heavy cream while stirring continuously. Continue to cook for 1-2 minutes until the caramel is smooth.
    4. Remove from heat and stir in the sea salt. Let the caramel sauce cool to room temperature.
2. **Prepare Frozen Yogurt Mixture**:
    1. In a large bowl, whisk together the Greek yogurt, heavy cream, granulated sugar, vanilla extract, and sea salt until the sugar is completely dissolved and the mixture is smooth.
3. **Churn Frozen Yogurt**:
    1. Pour the yogurt mixture into an ice cream maker and churn according to the manufacturer's instructions. This typically takes about 20-25 minutes.
4. **Swirl in Caramel**:
    1. Transfer half of the churned yogurt to an airtight container. Drizzle a few tablespoons of the cooled salted caramel sauce over the yogurt.
    2. Add the remaining yogurt on top and swirl with a knife or spatula to create a marble effect.
5. **Freeze**:
    1. Freeze the container for at least 2 hours, or until the frozen yogurt is firm.
6. **Serve**:

1. Scoop and enjoy your delicious Salted Caramel Swirl Frozen Yogurt!

Blueberry Basil Sorbet

Ingredients:

- 3 cups fresh blueberries (or frozen, thawed)
- 1 cup granulated sugar
- 1 cup water
- 1/4 cup freshly squeezed lemon juice
- 1/4 cup fresh basil leaves
- 1/2 teaspoon lemon zest (optional)

Instructions:

1. **Prepare Blueberry Mixture**:
    1. In a blender or food processor, combine the blueberries and granulated sugar. Blend until smooth.
2. **Make Simple Syrup**:
    1. In a small saucepan, combine the water and the remaining granulated sugar. Heat over medium heat, stirring occasionally until the sugar is fully dissolved. Remove from heat and let it cool to room temperature.
3. **Combine Mixtures**:
    1. Stir the cooled simple syrup into the blueberry puree. Add the freshly squeezed lemon juice and lemon zest (if using), and mix well.
4. **Infuse Basil**:
    1. Tear the basil leaves into smaller pieces and stir them into the blueberry mixture. Let it sit for about 30 minutes to allow the basil flavor to infuse.
5. **Strain Mixture**:
    1. After the basil has infused, strain the mixture through a fine-mesh sieve to remove the basil leaves, pressing with a spatula to extract as much liquid as possible.
6. **Freeze Mixture**:
    1. Pour the strained mixture into an ice cream maker and churn according to the manufacturer's instructions. This usually takes about 20-25 minutes, or until the sorbet reaches a soft-serve consistency.
7. **Freeze**:
    1. Transfer the churned sorbet to an airtight container. Freeze for at least 2 hours, or until it is firm.
8. **Serve**:
    1. Scoop and enjoy the refreshing and unique Blueberry Basil Sorbet!

Peanut Butter Cup Ice Cream

Ingredients:

For the Ice Cream Base:

- 2 cups heavy cream
- 1 cup whole milk
- 3/4 cup granulated sugar
- 1/2 cup creamy peanut butter
- 1 teaspoon vanilla extract
- 1/2 cup chopped peanut butter cups (plus extra for swirling)

For the Swirl:

- 1/2 cup peanut butter
- 1/4 cup heavy cream

Instructions:

1. **Prepare Ice Cream Base:**
    1. In a medium bowl, whisk together the granulated sugar and whole milk until the sugar is fully dissolved.
    2. Stir in the heavy cream, creamy peanut butter, and vanilla extract until smooth and well combined.
2. **Churn Ice Cream:**
    1. Pour the mixture into an ice cream maker and churn according to the manufacturer's instructions. This usually takes about 20-25 minutes, or until the ice cream reaches a soft-serve consistency.
    2. During the last 5 minutes of churning, add the chopped peanut butter cups to the ice cream maker.
3. **Prepare Swirl:**
    1. In a small saucepan, gently heat the peanut butter and heavy cream over low heat, stirring until smooth and combined. Remove from heat and let it cool slightly.
4. **Add Swirl:**
    1. Transfer the churned ice cream to an airtight container. Drizzle the peanut butter swirl over the ice cream, and use a knife or spatula to gently swirl it into the ice cream.
5. **Freeze:**
    1. Freeze the container for at least 2 hours, or until the ice cream is firm.
6. **Serve:**
    1. Scoop and enjoy your indulgent Peanut Butter Cup Ice Cream!

Pina Colada Sorbet

Ingredients:

- 2 cups fresh pineapple chunks (or canned pineapple in juice, drained)
- 1 cup coconut milk
- 1/2 cup granulated sugar
- 1/4 cup freshly squeezed lime juice
- 1/4 cup light rum (optional, for an adult version)
- 1/2 teaspoon vanilla extract

Instructions:

1. **Prepare Pineapple Puree**:
    1. In a blender or food processor, combine the pineapple chunks and granulated sugar. Blend until smooth.
2. **Combine Ingredients**:
    1. Add the coconut milk, freshly squeezed lime juice, and vanilla extract to the pineapple puree. If using, add the light rum. Blend until fully combined.
3. **Chill Mixture**:
    1. Refrigerate the mixture for at least 1 hour, or until it is thoroughly chilled.
4. **Churn Sorbet**:
    1. Pour the chilled mixture into an ice cream maker and churn according to the manufacturer's instructions. This usually takes about 20-25 minutes, or until the sorbet reaches a smooth, slushy texture.
5. **Freeze**:
    1. Transfer the churned sorbet to an airtight container. Freeze for at least 2 hours, or until it is firm.
6. **Serve**:
    1. Scoop and enjoy your refreshing Pina Colada Sorbet! For a tropical touch, garnish with a slice of pineapple or a maraschino cherry.

Matcha Green Tea Ice Cream

Ingredients:

- 2 cups heavy cream
- 1 cup whole milk
- 3/4 cup granulated sugar
- 2 tablespoons matcha green tea powder
- 1 teaspoon vanilla extract
- 1/4 teaspoon salt

Instructions:

1. **Prepare Matcha Mixture**:
    1. In a medium bowl, whisk together the granulated sugar and matcha green tea powder until well combined.
2. **Heat Dairy**:
    1. In a medium saucepan, combine the whole milk and heavy cream. Heat over medium heat until it is warmed and begins to steam, but do not let it boil.
3. **Combine Ingredients**:
    1. Gradually whisk the warm milk mixture into the bowl with the sugar and matcha mixture, stirring constantly to dissolve the matcha powder completely.
    2. Stir in the vanilla extract and salt.
4. **Chill Mixture**:
    1. Cover the bowl with plastic wrap and refrigerate the mixture for at least 1 hour, or until it is thoroughly chilled.
5. **Churn Ice Cream**:
    1. Pour the chilled mixture into an ice cream maker and churn according to the manufacturer's instructions. This usually takes about 20-25 minutes, or until the ice cream reaches a soft-serve consistency.
6. **Freeze**:
    1. Transfer the churned ice cream to an airtight container. Freeze for at least 2 hours, or until it is firm.
7. **Serve**:
    1. Scoop and enjoy your creamy, vibrant Matcha Green Tea Ice Cream!

Cookies and Cream Gelato

Ingredients:

- 2 cups whole milk
- 1 cup heavy cream
- 3/4 cup granulated sugar
- 4 large egg yolks
- 1 teaspoon vanilla extract
- 1 cup crushed chocolate sandwich cookies (e.g., Oreos)

Instructions:

1. **Prepare Custard Base:**
    1. In a medium saucepan, heat the whole milk and heavy cream over medium heat until it is warmed and begins to steam, but do not let it boil.
    2. In a separate bowl, whisk the granulated sugar and egg yolks together until pale and smooth.
2. **Temper Egg Yolks:**
    1. Gradually whisk a small amount of the warm milk mixture into the egg yolks to temper them. Continue to add the warm milk mixture in small increments, whisking constantly.
    2. Return the entire mixture to the saucepan. Cook over medium heat, stirring constantly, until the mixture thickens and coats the back of a spoon (about 5-7 minutes). Do not let it boil.
3. **Chill Custard Base:**
    1. Remove from heat and stir in the vanilla extract. Pour the mixture through a fine-mesh sieve into a clean bowl to remove any lumps. Allow the custard base to cool to room temperature.
    2. Cover the bowl and refrigerate for at least 2 hours, or until thoroughly chilled.
4. **Churn Gelato:**
    1. Pour the chilled custard base into an ice cream maker and churn according to the manufacturer's instructions. This usually takes about 20-25 minutes.
5. **Add Cookies:**
    1. During the last 5 minutes of churning, add the crushed chocolate sandwich cookies to the gelato maker, allowing them to mix evenly.
6. **Freeze:**
    1. Transfer the churned gelato to an airtight container. Freeze for at least 2 hours, or until it reaches a firm consistency.
7. **Serve:**
    1. Scoop and enjoy your rich and creamy Cookies and Cream Gelato!

Peach Melba Granita

Ingredients:

For the Peach Puree:

- 4 ripe peaches, peeled and pitted
- 1/4 cup granulated sugar
- 1 tablespoon freshly squeezed lemon juice

For the Raspberry Sauce:

- 1 cup fresh raspberries (or frozen, thawed)
- 1/4 cup granulated sugar
- 1 tablespoon freshly squeezed lemon juice

Instructions:

1. **Prepare Peach Puree:**
    1. In a blender or food processor, combine the peeled and pitted peaches with 1/4 cup granulated sugar and 1 tablespoon lemon juice. Blend until smooth.
    2. Pour the peach puree into a shallow baking dish.
2. **Prepare Raspberry Sauce:**
    1. In a small saucepan, combine the raspberries, 1/4 cup granulated sugar, and 1 tablespoon lemon juice. Cook over medium heat, stirring occasionally, until the raspberries break down and the mixture thickens slightly (about 5 minutes).
    2. Strain the raspberry sauce through a fine-mesh sieve to remove the seeds. Let it cool to room temperature.
3. **Freeze Peach Mixture:**
    1. Place the baking dish with the peach puree in the freezer. After 30 minutes, use a fork to scrape and stir the mixture to break up any ice crystals that have formed. Continue to scrape and stir every 30 minutes until the granita is fully frozen and has a fluffy, snow-like texture. This usually takes about 2-3 hours.
4. **Serve:**
    1. Scoop the peach granita into serving dishes or bowls. Drizzle with the raspberry sauce over the top.
5. **Garnish (Optional):**
    1. Garnish with fresh mint leaves or additional raspberries for a touch of elegance.
6. **Enjoy:**
    1. Serve immediately and enjoy the refreshing Peach Melba Granita!

Mocha Almond Fudge Ice Cream

Ingredients:

For the Ice Cream Base:

- 2 cups heavy cream
- 1 cup whole milk
- 3/4 cup granulated sugar
- 1/2 cup brewed espresso or strong coffee, cooled
- 1 teaspoon vanilla extract
- 1/2 cup cocoa powder

For the Fudge Swirl:

- 1/2 cup chocolate fudge sauce (store-bought or homemade)
- 1/4 cup chopped almonds (lightly toasted, if preferred)

Instructions:

1. **Prepare Ice Cream Base:**
    1. In a medium bowl, whisk together the granulated sugar and cocoa powder until well combined.
    2. In a separate bowl, mix the whole milk and heavy cream. Gradually whisk the milk mixture into the cocoa sugar mixture until smooth and the sugar is fully dissolved.
    3. Stir in the brewed espresso or coffee and vanilla extract.
2. **Chill Mixture:**
    1. Cover the bowl and refrigerate the mixture for at least 1 hour, or until it is thoroughly chilled.
3. **Churn Ice Cream:**
    1. Pour the chilled mixture into an ice cream maker and churn according to the manufacturer's instructions. This usually takes about 20-25 minutes, or until the ice cream reaches a soft-serve consistency.
4. **Add Fudge Swirl:**
    1. Transfer half of the churned ice cream to an airtight container. Drizzle half of the chocolate fudge sauce over the ice cream.
    2. Add the remaining ice cream on top, and drizzle with the remaining fudge sauce.
    3. Use a knife or spatula to gently swirl the fudge into the ice cream.
5. **Add Almonds:**
    1. Gently fold in the chopped almonds, or sprinkle them on top of the ice cream.
6. **Freeze:**
    1. Freeze the container for at least 2 hours, or until the ice cream is firm.
7. **Serve:**
    1. Scoop and enjoy your indulgent Mocha Almond Fudge Ice Cream!

Pineapple Coconut Frozen Smoothie

Ingredients:

- 2 cups fresh or frozen pineapple chunks
- 1 cup coconut milk
- 1/2 cup Greek yogurt (plain or vanilla)
- 1 tablespoon honey or agave syrup (adjust to taste)
- 1/2 cup ice cubes
- 1/4 cup shredded coconut (optional, for garnish)
- Pineapple slices or coconut flakes (optional, for garnish)

Instructions:

1. **Blend Ingredients:**
    1. In a blender, combine the pineapple chunks, coconut milk, Greek yogurt, honey (or agave syrup), and ice cubes.
    2. Blend on high speed until smooth and creamy. Adjust sweetness with more honey if desired.
2. **Serve:**
    1. Pour the smoothie into glasses.
3. **Garnish (Optional):**
    1. Sprinkle shredded coconut on top for added texture and flavor.
    2. Garnish with pineapple slices or coconut flakes if desired.
4. **Enjoy:**
    1. Serve immediately and enjoy your refreshing Pineapple Coconut Frozen Smoothie!

Raspberry White Chocolate Gelato

Ingredients:

For the Raspberry Puree:

- 2 cups fresh raspberries (or frozen, thawed)
- 1/4 cup granulated sugar
- 1 tablespoon freshly squeezed lemon juice

For the Gelato Base:

- 2 cups whole milk
- 1 cup heavy cream
- 3/4 cup granulated sugar
- 1/2 cup white chocolate chips
- 4 large egg yolks
- 1 teaspoon vanilla extract
- A pinch of salt

Instructions:

1. **Prepare Raspberry Puree:**
    1. In a blender or food processor, combine the raspberries, granulated sugar, and lemon juice. Blend until smooth.
    2. Strain the raspberry puree through a fine-mesh sieve to remove the seeds. Set aside.
2. **Prepare White Chocolate:**
    1. In a small saucepan over low heat, gently melt the white chocolate chips, stirring constantly until smooth. Remove from heat and let it cool slightly.
3. **Prepare Gelato Base:**
    1. In a medium saucepan, heat the whole milk and heavy cream over medium heat until it starts to steam but does not boil.
    2. In a separate bowl, whisk together the granulated sugar and egg yolks until pale and smooth.
    3. Gradually whisk the warm milk mixture into the egg yolks to temper them. Return the mixture to the saucepan and cook over medium heat, stirring constantly, until the custard thickens and coats the back of a spoon (about 5-7 minutes). Do not let it boil.
    4. Remove from heat and stir in the melted white chocolate, vanilla extract, and a pinch of salt. Stir until well combined and smooth.
4. **Combine with Raspberry Puree:**
    1. Allow the custard base to cool to room temperature. Once cooled, stir in the raspberry puree.
5. **Chill Mixture:**

1. Cover the mixture and refrigerate for at least 2 hours, or until it is thoroughly chilled.

6. **Churn Gelato:**
    1. Pour the chilled mixture into an ice cream maker and churn according to the manufacturer's instructions. This usually takes about 20-25 minutes, or until the gelato reaches a smooth, creamy texture.
7. **Freeze:**
    1. Transfer the churned gelato to an airtight container. Freeze for at least 2 hours, or until it is firm.
8. **Serve:**
    1. Scoop and enjoy your luxurious Raspberry White Chocolate Gelato!

Lemon Basil Sorbet

Ingredients:

- 1 cup freshly squeezed lemon juice (about 4-6 lemons)
- 1 cup granulated sugar
- 1 cup water
- 1/2 cup fresh basil leaves, packed
- 1 tablespoon lemon zest (optional, for extra flavor)
- A pinch of salt

Instructions:

1. **Make Simple Syrup:**
    1. In a small saucepan, combine the water and granulated sugar. Heat over medium heat, stirring occasionally, until the sugar is completely dissolved. Remove from heat and let it cool to room temperature.
2. **Infuse Basil:**
    1. Once the simple syrup has cooled, add the fresh basil leaves. Let it steep for about 30 minutes to infuse the basil flavor.
3. **Prepare Lemon Mixture:**
    1. Strain the basil-infused syrup through a fine-mesh sieve into a large bowl, discarding the basil leaves.
    2. Stir in the freshly squeezed lemon juice and lemon zest (if using). Add a pinch of salt and mix well.
4. **Chill Mixture:**
    1. Refrigerate the mixture for at least 1 hour, or until it is thoroughly chilled.
5. **Churn Sorbet:**
    1. Pour the chilled mixture into an ice cream maker and churn according to the manufacturer's instructions. This usually takes about 20-25 minutes, or until the sorbet reaches a smooth, slushy texture.
6. **Freeze:**
    1. Transfer the churned sorbet to an airtight container. Freeze for at least 2 hours, or until it is firm.
7. **Serve:**
    1. Scoop and enjoy your refreshing Lemon Basil Sorbet! Garnish with a fresh basil leaf or a lemon twist if desired.

Hazelnut Coffee Ice Cream

Ingredients:

For the Ice Cream Base:

- 2 cups heavy cream
- 1 cup whole milk
- 3/4 cup granulated sugar
- 1/2 cup hazelnut paste or finely ground hazelnuts
- 1/2 cup brewed strong coffee (cooled)
- 1 teaspoon vanilla extract
- 1/4 teaspoon salt

For the Swirl (Optional):

- 1/4 cup chocolate hazelnut spread (such as Nutella)

Instructions:

1. **Prepare Ice Cream Base:**
    1. In a medium bowl, whisk together the granulated sugar and whole milk until the sugar is fully dissolved.
    2. Stir in the heavy cream, hazelnut paste (or ground hazelnuts), brewed coffee, vanilla extract, and salt until smooth and well combined.
2. **Chill Mixture:**
    1. Cover the bowl and refrigerate the mixture for at least 1 hour, or until it is thoroughly chilled.
3. **Churn Ice Cream:**
    1. Pour the chilled mixture into an ice cream maker and churn according to the manufacturer's instructions. This usually takes about 20-25 minutes, or until the ice cream reaches a soft-serve consistency.
4. **Add Swirl (Optional):**
    1. If using a chocolate hazelnut spread, gently swirl it into the churned ice cream by spooning it in and lightly folding with a knife or spatula to create a marbled effect.
5. **Freeze:**
    1. Transfer the churned ice cream to an airtight container. Freeze for at least 2 hours, or until the ice cream is firm.
6. **Serve:**
    1. Scoop and enjoy your rich and creamy Hazelnut Coffee Ice Cream!

Blackberry Mint Frozen Yogurt

Ingredients:

For the Blackberry Puree:

- 2 cups fresh blackberries (or frozen, thawed)
- 1/4 cup granulated sugar
- 1 tablespoon freshly squeezed lemon juice

For the Yogurt Mixture:

- 2 cups plain Greek yogurt (full-fat or 2%)
- 1 cup heavy cream
- 1/2 cup granulated sugar
- 1 teaspoon vanilla extract
- 1/4 cup fresh mint leaves, finely chopped

Instructions:

1. **Prepare Blackberry Puree:**
    1. In a blender or food processor, combine the blackberries, granulated sugar, and lemon juice. Blend until smooth.
    2. Strain the blackberry puree through a fine-mesh sieve to remove seeds. Set aside.
2. **Prepare Yogurt Mixture:**
    1. In a large bowl, whisk together the Greek yogurt and granulated sugar until the sugar is fully dissolved.
    2. Stir in the heavy cream, vanilla extract, and finely chopped mint leaves. Mix well.
3. **Combine Mixtures:**
    1. Gently fold the blackberry puree into the yogurt mixture, creating a swirl effect. Be careful not to overmix.
4. **Chill Mixture:**
    1. Cover the bowl and refrigerate the mixture for at least 1 hour, or until it is thoroughly chilled.
5. **Churn Frozen Yogurt:**
    1. Pour the chilled mixture into an ice cream maker and churn according to the manufacturer's instructions. This usually takes about 20-25 minutes, or until the frozen yogurt reaches a smooth, creamy texture.
6. **Freeze:**
    1. Transfer the churned frozen yogurt to an airtight container. Freeze for at least 2 hours, or until it is firm.
7. **Serve:**
    1. Scoop and enjoy your refreshing Blackberry Mint Frozen Yogurt! Garnish with a few fresh mint leaves or extra blackberries if desired.

Cinnamon Roll Ice Cream

Ingredients:

For the Ice Cream Base:

- 2 cups heavy cream
- 1 cup whole milk
- 3/4 cup granulated sugar
- 1 teaspoon vanilla extract
- 1 teaspoon ground cinnamon
- 1/4 teaspoon ground nutmeg
- 1/4 teaspoon salt

For the Cinnamon Swirl:

- 1/2 cup cinnamon roll filling (store-bought or homemade)
- 1/2 cup chopped cinnamon roll pieces (optional, for added texture)

For Homemade Cinnamon Roll Filling (Optional):

- 1/4 cup unsalted butter, softened
- 1/4 cup brown sugar
- 1 tablespoon ground cinnamon
- 1/4 cup all-purpose flour

Instructions:

1. **Prepare Cinnamon Roll Filling (if making from scratch):**
    1. In a small bowl, combine the softened butter, brown sugar, ground cinnamon, and flour. Mix until it forms a crumbly paste. Set aside.
2. **Prepare Ice Cream Base:**
    1. In a large bowl, whisk together the granulated sugar, ground cinnamon, ground nutmeg, and salt.
    2. Stir in the whole milk and heavy cream until the sugar is fully dissolved.
    3. Add the vanilla extract and mix well.
3. **Chill Mixture:**
    1. Cover the bowl and refrigerate the mixture for at least 1 hour, or until it is thoroughly chilled.
4. **Churn Ice Cream:**
    1. Pour the chilled mixture into an ice cream maker and churn according to the manufacturer's instructions. This usually takes about 20-25 minutes, or until the ice cream reaches a soft-serve consistency.
5. **Add Cinnamon Swirl:**
    1. Gently fold in the cinnamon roll filling and chopped cinnamon roll pieces (if using) into the churned ice cream, creating a swirl effect. Be careful not to overmix.

6. **Freeze:**
    1. Transfer the churned ice cream to an airtight container. Freeze for at least 2 hours, or until the ice cream is firm.
7. **Serve:**
    1. Scoop and enjoy your creamy and indulgent Cinnamon Roll Ice Cream! For extra flavor, you can drizzle with additional cinnamon roll filling or sprinkle with a little extra ground cinnamon.

Watermelon Mint Granita

Ingredients:

- 4 cups seedless watermelon, cut into chunks
- 1/2 cup granulated sugar
- 1/4 cup freshly squeezed lime juice (about 2 limes)
- 1/4 cup fresh mint leaves, packed
- 1/4 cup water

Instructions:

1. **Prepare Watermelon Puree:**
    1. In a blender or food processor, combine the watermelon chunks and granulated sugar. Blend until smooth.
2. **Infuse Mint:**
    1. In a small saucepan, heat the water until just about to boil. Remove from heat and add the fresh mint leaves. Let it steep for about 5 minutes to infuse the mint flavor.
    2. Strain the mint-infused water through a fine-mesh sieve to remove the mint leaves.
3. **Combine Ingredients:**
    1. Stir the mint-infused water and freshly squeezed lime juice into the watermelon puree. Mix well.
4. **Freeze Mixture:**
    1. Pour the mixture into a shallow baking dish or a large tray.
    2. Place in the freezer and freeze for about 1 hour. After 1 hour, use a fork to scrape and stir the mixture to break up any ice crystals that have formed.
    3. Continue to freeze and scrape every 30 minutes, for about 2-3 hours, until the granita is fully frozen and has a fluffy, snow-like texture.
5. **Serve:**
    1. Use a fork to fluff the granita before serving. Scoop into glasses or bowls.
6. **Garnish (Optional):**
    1. Garnish with fresh mint leaves or a small watermelon wedge if desired.
7. **Enjoy:**
    1. Serve immediately and enjoy the refreshing Watermelon Mint Granita!

Pumpkin Spice Frozen Custard

Ingredients:

For the Custard Base:

- 2 cups heavy cream
- 1 cup whole milk
- 3/4 cup granulated sugar
- 4 large egg yolks
- 1 cup canned pumpkin puree (not pumpkin pie filling)
- 1 teaspoon vanilla extract
- 1 teaspoon ground cinnamon
- 1/2 teaspoon ground ginger
- 1/4 teaspoon ground nutmeg
- 1/4 teaspoon ground cloves
- A pinch of salt

Instructions:

1. **Prepare Custard Base:**
    1. In a medium saucepan, heat the whole milk and heavy cream over medium heat until it starts to steam but does not boil.
    2. In a separate bowl, whisk together the granulated sugar and egg yolks until pale and smooth.
    3. Gradually whisk the warm milk mixture into the egg yolks to temper them. Return the mixture to the saucepan and cook over medium heat, stirring constantly, until the custard thickens and coats the back of a spoon (about 5-7 minutes). Do not let it boil.
2. **Add Pumpkin and Spices:**
    1. Remove the saucepan from heat and stir in the canned pumpkin puree, vanilla extract, ground cinnamon, ground ginger, ground nutmeg, ground cloves, and a pinch of salt. Mix until fully combined and smooth.
3. **Chill Custard Base:**
    1. Pour the custard base through a fine-mesh sieve into a clean bowl to remove any lumps. Let it cool to room temperature.
    2. Cover the bowl and refrigerate for at least 2 hours, or until it is thoroughly chilled.
4. **Churn Custard:**
    1. Pour the chilled custard base into an ice cream maker and churn according to the manufacturer's instructions. This usually takes about 20-25 minutes, or until the custard reaches a smooth, creamy texture.
5. **Freeze:**
    1. Transfer the churned custard to an airtight container. Freeze for at least 2 hours, or until the custard is firm.
6. **Serve:**

1. Scoop and enjoy your creamy, spiced Pumpkin Spice Frozen Custard! For an extra touch, top with a sprinkle of cinnamon or a dollop of whipped cream.

Chocolate Raspberry Sorbet

Ingredients:

- 2 cups fresh raspberries (or frozen, thawed)
- 1 cup granulated sugar
- 1 cup water
- 1/2 cup unsweetened cocoa powder
- 1 tablespoon lemon juice
- 1 teaspoon vanilla extract
- A pinch of salt

Instructions:

1. **Prepare Raspberry Puree:**
    1. In a blender or food processor, combine the raspberries and granulated sugar. Blend until smooth.
    2. Strain the raspberry puree through a fine-mesh sieve to remove the seeds. Set aside.
2. **Make Chocolate Syrup:**
    1. In a small saucepan, whisk together the water and cocoa powder over medium heat until the cocoa powder is fully dissolved and the mixture is smooth. Bring to a simmer and cook for 2-3 minutes, stirring constantly.
    2. Remove from heat and let the chocolate syrup cool to room temperature.
3. **Combine Mixtures:**
    1. Stir the cooled chocolate syrup into the raspberry puree until well combined.
    2. Add the lemon juice, vanilla extract, and a pinch of salt. Mix well.
4. **Chill Mixture:**
    1. Cover the mixture and refrigerate for at least 1 hour, or until it is thoroughly chilled.
5. **Churn Sorbet:**
    1. Pour the chilled mixture into an ice cream maker and churn according to the manufacturer's instructions. This usually takes about 20-25 minutes, or until the sorbet reaches a smooth, slushy texture.
6. **Freeze:**
    1. Transfer the churned sorbet to an airtight container. Freeze for at least 2 hours, or until it is firm.
7. **Serve:**
    1. Scoop and enjoy your rich and refreshing Chocolate Raspberry Sorbet! For an extra touch, garnish with fresh raspberries or a sprig of mint if desired.

Almond Joy Gelato

Ingredients:

For the Gelato Base:

- 2 cups whole milk
- 1 cup heavy cream
- 3/4 cup granulated sugar
- 1/2 cup almond paste or finely ground almonds
- 1 teaspoon vanilla extract
- 1/2 cup unsweetened cocoa powder
- 1/4 teaspoon salt

For the Swirl:

- 1/2 cup sweetened shredded coconut
- 1/2 cup chopped almonds (lightly toasted if desired)
- 1/2 cup chocolate fudge sauce (store-bought or homemade)

Instructions:

1. **Prepare Gelato Base:**
    1. In a medium saucepan, heat the whole milk and heavy cream over medium heat until it begins to steam but does not boil.
    2. In a separate bowl, whisk together the granulated sugar, almond paste (or ground almonds), cocoa powder, and salt.
    3. Gradually whisk the warm milk mixture into the almond mixture until smooth and fully combined.
    4. Return the mixture to the saucepan and cook over medium heat, stirring constantly, until the mixture thickens slightly (about 5-7 minutes). Do not let it boil.
    5. Remove from heat and stir in the vanilla extract.
2. **Chill Mixture:**
    1. Pour the mixture through a fine-mesh sieve into a clean bowl to remove any lumps. Allow it to cool to room temperature.
    2. Cover and refrigerate for at least 2 hours, or until thoroughly chilled.
3. **Churn Gelato:**
    1. Pour the chilled mixture into an ice cream maker and churn according to the manufacturer's instructions. This usually takes about 20-25 minutes, or until the gelato reaches a smooth, creamy texture.
4. **Add Swirl:**
    1. During the last 5 minutes of churning, gently fold in the shredded coconut and chopped almonds.
    2. Once the gelato is almost finished churning, swirl in the chocolate fudge sauce to create a marbled effect.

5. **Freeze:**
    1. Transfer the churned gelato to an airtight container. Freeze for at least 2 hours, or until firm.
6. **Serve:**
    1. Scoop and enjoy your indulgent Almond Joy Gelato! For extra flair, garnish with additional toasted almonds or a drizzle of extra fudge sauce if desired.

Key Lime Pie Frozen Yogurt

Ingredients:

For the Frozen Yogurt:

- 2 cups plain Greek yogurt (full-fat or 2%)
- 1 cup heavy cream
- 1/2 cup granulated sugar
- 1/2 cup freshly squeezed lime juice (about 4-6 limes)
- 2 tablespoons lime zest (from about 2 limes)
- 1 teaspoon vanilla extract
- A pinch of salt

For the Graham Cracker Crust Swirl:

- 1 cup graham cracker crumbs
- 2 tablespoons granulated sugar
- 3 tablespoons unsalted butter, melted

Instructions:

1. **Prepare Graham Cracker Crust Swirl:**
    1. In a small bowl, combine the graham cracker crumbs, granulated sugar, and melted butter. Mix until the crumbs are well coated and the mixture resembles coarse crumbs. Set aside.
2. **Prepare Frozen Yogurt Base:**
    1. In a large bowl, whisk together the granulated sugar and Greek yogurt until the sugar is fully dissolved.
    2. Stir in the heavy cream, freshly squeezed lime juice, lime zest, vanilla extract, and a pinch of salt. Mix until well combined.
3. **Chill Mixture:**
    1. Cover the mixture and refrigerate for at least 1 hour, or until it is thoroughly chilled.
4. **Churn Frozen Yogurt:**
    1. Pour the chilled mixture into an ice cream maker and churn according to the manufacturer's instructions. This usually takes about 20-25 minutes, or until the frozen yogurt reaches a smooth, creamy texture.
5. **Add Graham Cracker Crust Swirl:**
    1. During the last 5 minutes of churning, gently fold in the graham cracker crust mixture. This will create a swirled effect throughout the frozen yogurt.
6. **Freeze:**
    1. Transfer the churned frozen yogurt to an airtight container. Freeze for at least 2 hours, or until it is firm.
7. **Serve:**

1. Scoop and enjoy your refreshing Key Lime Pie Frozen Yogurt! For an extra touch, garnish with additional graham cracker crumbs or a thin lime slice if desired.

Espresso Affogato

Ingredients:

- 2 scoops vanilla ice cream (or gelato)
- 1 shot (1 ounce) hot espresso
- 1 tablespoon coffee liqueur (optional, for extra depth of flavor)
- Shaved chocolate or cocoa powder (optional, for garnish)
- Fresh mint leaves (optional, for garnish)

Instructions:

1. **Prepare Espresso:**
    1. Brew a shot of espresso using your preferred method (espresso machine, stovetop espresso maker, etc.). Keep it hot.
2. **Scoop Ice Cream:**
    1. Place 2 scoops of vanilla ice cream or gelato into a serving glass or bowl.
3. **Add Espresso:**
    1. Pour the hot espresso over the ice cream, allowing the rich coffee to gently melt and combine with the creamy ice cream.
4. **Optional Enhancements:**
    1. If using, drizzle 1 tablespoon of coffee liqueur over the espresso and ice cream for an extra layer of flavor.
    2. Garnish with shaved chocolate or a light dusting of cocoa powder.
    3. Add a few fresh mint leaves for a touch of color and freshness.
5. **Serve Immediately:**
    1. Serve immediately, while the espresso is still hot and the ice cream is cold, creating a delightful contrast in temperatures.

Enjoy your classic and indulgent Espresso Affogato!

Cherry Vanilla Ice Cream

Ingredients:

For the Cherry Swirl:

- 2 cups fresh or frozen cherries, pitted and halved
- 1/2 cup granulated sugar
- 1 tablespoon lemon juice

For the Vanilla Ice Cream Base:

- 2 cups heavy cream
- 1 cup whole milk
- 3/4 cup granulated sugar
- 1 tablespoon vanilla extract
- 1/4 teaspoon salt

Instructions:

1. **Prepare Cherry Swirl:**
    1. In a medium saucepan, combine the cherries, granulated sugar, and lemon juice.
    2. Cook over medium heat, stirring occasionally, until the cherries break down and the mixture thickens slightly (about 10-15 minutes). The mixture should be chunky but not overly thick.
    3. Let the cherry mixture cool completely. You can refrigerate it to speed up the cooling process.
2. **Prepare Vanilla Ice Cream Base:**
    1. In a large bowl, whisk together the granulated sugar and whole milk until the sugar is fully dissolved.
    2. Stir in the heavy cream, vanilla extract, and salt. Mix until well combined.
3. **Chill Mixture:**
    1. Cover the vanilla ice cream base and refrigerate for at least 1 hour, or until it is thoroughly chilled.
4. **Churn Ice Cream:**
    1. Pour the chilled vanilla ice cream base into an ice cream maker and churn according to the manufacturer's instructions. This usually takes about 20-25 minutes, or until the ice cream reaches a soft-serve consistency.
5. **Add Cherry Swirl:**
    1. Transfer the churned ice cream to an airtight container.
    2. Gently fold in the cherry mixture, creating a swirl effect. Be careful not to overmix; you want ribbons of cherry throughout the ice cream.
6. **Freeze:**
    1. Freeze the ice cream for at least 2 hours, or until it is firm.
7. **Serve:**

1. Scoop and enjoy your delicious Cherry Vanilla Ice Cream! For added flair, garnish with a few whole cherries or a mint leaf if desired.

Tropical Fruit Sorbet

Ingredients:

- 2 cups fresh pineapple chunks
- 1 cup mango chunks (fresh or frozen)
- 1 cup fresh papaya chunks (or substitute with additional mango)
- 1/2 cup granulated sugar
- 1/2 cup freshly squeezed lime juice (about 3-4 limes)
- 1/4 cup water
- 1 tablespoon honey or agave syrup (optional, for added sweetness)

Instructions:

1. **Prepare Fruit Puree:**
    1. In a blender or food processor, combine the pineapple chunks, mango chunks, and papaya chunks. Blend until smooth.
2. **Sweeten and Flavor:**
    1. In a small bowl, mix the granulated sugar with the water until the sugar is dissolved. Stir this sugar syrup into the fruit puree.
    2. Add the freshly squeezed lime juice and honey or agave syrup (if using). Mix well.
3. **Chill Mixture:**
    1. Cover the mixture and refrigerate for at least 1 hour, or until it is thoroughly chilled.
4. **Churn Sorbet:**
    1. Pour the chilled mixture into an ice cream maker and churn according to the manufacturer's instructions. This usually takes about 20-25 minutes, or until the sorbet reaches a smooth, slushy texture.
5. **Freeze:**
    1. Transfer the churned sorbet to an airtight container. Freeze for at least 2 hours, or until it is firm.
6. **Serve:**
    1. Scoop and enjoy your refreshing Tropical Fruit Sorbet! For an extra touch, garnish with fresh mint leaves or a slice of tropical fruit.

Enjoy the vibrant flavors of the tropics in every spoonful!

Nutella Swirl Gelato

Ingredients:

For the Gelato Base:

- 2 cups whole milk
- 1 cup heavy cream
- 3/4 cup granulated sugar
- 1/2 cup Nutella or other chocolate-hazelnut spread
- 4 large egg yolks
- 1 teaspoon vanilla extract
- A pinch of salt

Instructions:

1. **Prepare Gelato Base:**
    1. In a medium saucepan, heat the whole milk and heavy cream over medium heat until it begins to steam but does not boil.
    2. In a separate bowl, whisk together the granulated sugar and egg yolks until pale and smooth.
    3. Gradually whisk the warm milk mixture into the egg yolks to temper them. Return the mixture to the saucepan and cook over medium heat, stirring constantly, until it thickens slightly and coats the back of a spoon (about 5-7 minutes). Do not let it boil.
    4. Remove from heat and stir in the Nutella until fully incorporated and smooth. Add the vanilla extract and a pinch of salt. Mix well.
2. **Chill Mixture:**
    1. Pour the mixture through a fine-mesh sieve into a clean bowl to remove any lumps. Allow it to cool to room temperature.
    2. Cover and refrigerate for at least 2 hours, or until thoroughly chilled.
3. **Churn Gelato:**
    1. Pour the chilled mixture into an ice cream maker and churn according to the manufacturer's instructions. This usually takes about 20-25 minutes, or until the gelato reaches a smooth, creamy texture.
4. **Add Nutella Swirl:**
    1. During the last 5 minutes of churning, gently swirl in additional Nutella (about 1/4 cup) to create ribbons of Nutella throughout the gelato.
5. **Freeze:**
    1. Transfer the churned gelato to an airtight container. Freeze for at least 2 hours, or until firm.
6. **Serve:**
    1. Scoop and enjoy your rich and creamy Nutella Swirl Gelato! For an extra touch, you can drizzle some extra Nutella on top or sprinkle with chopped hazelnuts if desired.

Indulge in the delicious blend of creamy gelato and luscious Nutella swirl!

Spiced Apple Frozen Smoothie

Ingredients:

- 2 cups frozen apple chunks (or fresh apples, peeled and chopped, frozen)
- 1 cup plain Greek yogurt (or vanilla yogurt for added sweetness)
- 1/2 cup apple juice or cider
- 1/2 cup milk (dairy or non-dairy)
- 1 tablespoon honey or maple syrup (adjust to taste)
- 1/2 teaspoon ground cinnamon
- 1/4 teaspoon ground nutmeg
- A pinch of ground cloves (optional)
- 1/2 teaspoon vanilla extract
- Ice cubes (optional, for a thicker smoothie)

Instructions:

1. **Prepare Ingredients:**
    1. If using fresh apples, peel, chop, and freeze them in advance. For a smoother consistency, you can also add a few ice cubes to the blender.
2. **Blend Smoothie:**
    1. In a blender, combine the frozen apple chunks, Greek yogurt, apple juice or cider, milk, honey or maple syrup, ground cinnamon, ground nutmeg, ground cloves (if using), and vanilla extract.
    2. Blend until smooth and creamy. If the smoothie is too thick, add a little more milk or apple juice to reach your desired consistency.
3. **Adjust Sweetness and Spices:**
    1. Taste the smoothie and adjust sweetness with additional honey or maple syrup if needed. You can also add more spices to suit your taste.
4. **Serve:**
    1. Pour the smoothie into glasses. For an extra touch, you can sprinkle a little extra ground cinnamon on top.
5. **Garnish (Optional):**
    1. Garnish with a cinnamon stick or a thin apple slice on the rim of the glass for a decorative touch.

Enjoy your refreshing and spiced apple smoothie, perfect for a cool treat or a nutritious snack!

Hibiscus Raspberry Sorbet

Ingredients:

- 2 cups fresh raspberries (or frozen, thawed)
- 1 cup granulated sugar
- 1 cup water
- 2 tablespoons dried hibiscus flowers (or 1/4 cup hibiscus tea, brewed and cooled)
- 1/4 cup freshly squeezed lemon juice (about 2 lemons)
- 1 teaspoon lemon zest (optional, for extra flavor)
- A pinch of salt

Instructions:

1. **Prepare Hibiscus Infusion:**
    1. In a small saucepan, bring 1 cup of water to a boil.
    2. Remove from heat and add the dried hibiscus flowers. Let steep for about 5 minutes.
    3. Strain the mixture through a fine-mesh sieve to remove the flowers, and let the hibiscus tea cool to room temperature.
2. **Prepare Raspberry Puree:**
    1. In a blender or food processor, combine the raspberries and granulated sugar. Blend until smooth.
    2. Strain the raspberry puree through a fine-mesh sieve to remove the seeds.
3. **Combine Mixtures:**
    1. Stir the cooled hibiscus tea into the raspberry puree.
    2. Add the freshly squeezed lemon juice and lemon zest (if using). Mix well.
4. **Chill Mixture:**
    1. Cover the mixture and refrigerate for at least 1 hour, or until it is thoroughly chilled.
5. **Churn Sorbet:**
    1. Pour the chilled mixture into an ice cream maker and churn according to the manufacturer's instructions. This usually takes about 20-25 minutes, or until the sorbet reaches a smooth, slushy texture.
6. **Freeze:**
    1. Transfer the churned sorbet to an airtight container. Freeze for at least 2 hours, or until it is firm.
7. **Serve:**
    1. Scoop and enjoy your vibrant and refreshing Hibiscus Raspberry Sorbet! For an extra touch, garnish with a few fresh raspberries or a sprig of mint.

Enjoy the floral and fruity blend of hibiscus and raspberry in this delightful sorbet!

Caramel Macchiato Ice Cream

Ingredients:

For the Ice Cream Base:

- 2 cups whole milk
- 1 cup heavy cream
- 3/4 cup granulated sugar
- 1/2 cup strong brewed coffee, cooled
- 1 teaspoon vanilla extract
- A pinch of salt

For the Caramel Swirl:

- 1/2 cup caramel sauce (store-bought or homemade)
- 1 tablespoon coffee liqueur (optional, for extra depth of flavor)

Instructions:

1. **Prepare Ice Cream Base:**
    1. In a medium saucepan, heat the whole milk and heavy cream over medium heat until it begins to steam but does not boil.
    2. In a separate bowl, whisk together the granulated sugar and a pinch of salt until the sugar is fully dissolved.
    3. Gradually whisk the warm milk mixture into the sugar mixture until smooth. Stir in the cooled brewed coffee and vanilla extract.
2. **Chill Mixture:**
    1. Pour the mixture through a fine-mesh sieve into a clean bowl to remove any lumps.
    2. Cover and refrigerate for at least 1-2 hours, or until thoroughly chilled.
3. **Churn Ice Cream:**
    1. Pour the chilled mixture into an ice cream maker and churn according to the manufacturer's instructions. This usually takes about 20-25 minutes, or until the ice cream reaches a soft-serve consistency.
4. **Add Caramel Swirl:**
    1. During the last 5 minutes of churning, gently fold in the caramel sauce to create a swirl effect. If using, also add the coffee liqueur for an extra layer of flavor.
5. **Freeze:**
    1. Transfer the churned ice cream to an airtight container. Freeze for at least 2 hours, or until the ice cream is firm.
6. **Serve:**
    1. Scoop and enjoy your creamy Caramel Macchiato Ice Cream! For an added touch, you can drizzle extra caramel sauce on top or sprinkle with a bit of sea salt.

Indulge in the delicious blend of coffee and caramel with each creamy bite!

Lemon Blueberry Cheesecake Gelato

Ingredients:

For the Lemon Blueberry Cheesecake Base:

- 2 cups whole milk
- 1 cup heavy cream
- 3/4 cup granulated sugar
- 1 cup cream cheese, softened
- 1/2 cup sour cream
- 1/4 cup freshly squeezed lemon juice (about 2 lemons)
- 1 tablespoon lemon zest
- 1 teaspoon vanilla extract
- A pinch of salt

For the Blueberry Swirl:

- 1 1/2 cups fresh or frozen blueberries
- 1/4 cup granulated sugar
- 1 tablespoon lemon juice
- 1/4 cup water

For the Cheesecake Crust Pieces:

- 1/2 cup graham cracker crumbs
- 2 tablespoons granulated sugar
- 3 tablespoons unsalted butter, melted

Instructions:

1. **Prepare Blueberry Swirl:**
    1. In a small saucepan, combine the blueberries, granulated sugar, lemon juice, and water.
    2. Cook over medium heat, stirring occasionally, until the blueberries break down and the mixture thickens slightly (about 10-15 minutes).
    3. Let the blueberry mixture cool completely. You can refrigerate it to speed up the cooling process.
2. **Prepare Cheesecake Base:**
    1. In a medium saucepan, heat the whole milk and heavy cream over medium heat until it begins to steam but does not boil.
    2. In a large bowl, whisk together the granulated sugar, softened cream cheese, sour cream, lemon juice, lemon zest, vanilla extract, and a pinch of salt until smooth and well combined.
    3. Gradually whisk the warm milk mixture into the cream cheese mixture until smooth and combined.

3. **Chill Mixture:**
    1. Cover the mixture and refrigerate for at least 1-2 hours, or until thoroughly chilled.
4. **Prepare Cheesecake Crust Pieces:**
    1. In a small bowl, mix the graham cracker crumbs, granulated sugar, and melted butter until the crumbs are evenly coated and resemble coarse crumbs.
5. **Churn Gelato:**
    1. Pour the chilled cheesecake mixture into an ice cream maker and churn according to the manufacturer's instructions. This usually takes about 20-25 minutes, or until the gelato reaches a smooth, creamy texture.
6. **Add Swirls and Crust Pieces:**
    1. During the last 5 minutes of churning, gently fold in the blueberry swirl to create ribbons throughout the gelato.
    2. Add the cheesecake crust pieces, folding them in gently.
7. **Freeze:**
    1. Transfer the churned gelato to an airtight container. Freeze for at least 2 hours, or until firm.
8. **Serve:**
    1. Scoop and enjoy your delectable Lemon Blueberry Cheesecake Gelato! For an extra touch, you can garnish with additional blueberry sauce or a sprinkle of graham cracker crumbs.

Delight in the creamy blend of lemon, blueberry, and cheesecake with every spoonful!

White Chocolate Ginger Frozen Yogurt

Ingredients:

For the Frozen Yogurt Base:

- 2 cups plain Greek yogurt (full-fat or 2%)
- 1 cup heavy cream
- 3/4 cup granulated sugar
- 1/2 cup white chocolate chips or finely chopped white chocolate
- 1 tablespoon freshly grated ginger (or 1 teaspoon ground ginger)
- 1 teaspoon vanilla extract
- A pinch of salt

For the Ginger Swirl:

- 1/4 cup finely chopped crystallized ginger
- 1 tablespoon honey or maple syrup (optional, for extra sweetness)

Instructions:

1. **Melt White Chocolate:**
    1. In a microwave-safe bowl, melt the white chocolate chips in 20-30 second intervals, stirring in between, until completely smooth. Allow to cool slightly.
2. **Prepare Frozen Yogurt Base:**
    1. In a large bowl, whisk together the granulated sugar and Greek yogurt until the sugar is fully dissolved.
    2. Stir in the heavy cream, melted white chocolate, freshly grated ginger, vanilla extract, and a pinch of salt. Mix until well combined.
3. **Chill Mixture:**
    1. Cover the mixture and refrigerate for at least 1 hour, or until it is thoroughly chilled.
4. **Churn Frozen Yogurt:**
    1. Pour the chilled mixture into an ice cream maker and churn according to the manufacturer's instructions. This usually takes about 20-25 minutes, or until the frozen yogurt reaches a soft-serve consistency.
5. **Add Ginger Swirl:**
    1. During the last 5 minutes of churning, gently fold in the finely chopped crystallized ginger and, if using, the honey or maple syrup.
6. **Freeze:**
    1. Transfer the churned frozen yogurt to an airtight container. Freeze for at least 2 hours, or until it is firm.
7. **Serve:**
    1. Scoop and enjoy your creamy and flavorful White Chocolate Ginger Frozen Yogurt! For an extra touch, you can garnish with additional chopped crystallized ginger or a drizzle of melted white chocolate.

Experience the harmonious blend of sweet white chocolate and spicy ginger in each refreshing bite!

Classic Strawberry Ice Cream

Ingredients:

- 2 cups fresh strawberries, hulled and sliced
- 3/4 cup granulated sugar
- 1 cup whole milk
- 1 cup heavy cream
- 1 teaspoon vanilla extract
- 1 tablespoon lemon juice (optional, to enhance strawberry flavor)
- A pinch of salt

Instructions:

1. **Prepare Strawberry Puree:**
    1. In a blender or food processor, combine the fresh strawberries and 1/4 cup of granulated sugar. Blend until smooth.
    2. Taste the mixture and adjust sweetness if needed by adding more sugar. You can also add a tablespoon of lemon juice to enhance the flavor of the strawberries.
2. **Chill Strawberry Mixture:**
    1. Pour the strawberry puree into a bowl and refrigerate while you prepare the rest
    2. of the mixture.
3. **Prepare Ice Cream Base:**
    1. In a medium saucepan, heat the whole milk and remaining 1/2 cup of granulated sugar over medium heat until it begins to steam but does not boil.
    2. Remove from heat and stir in the heavy cream, vanilla extract, and a pinch of salt.
4. **Combine Mixtures:**
    1. Allow the milk and cream mixture to cool to room temperature.
    2. Once cooled, stir in the chilled strawberry puree until fully combined.
5. **Chill Mixture:**
    1. Cover the mixture and refrigerate for at least 1-2 hours, or until it is thoroughly chilled.
6. **Churn Ice Cream:**
    1. Pour the chilled mixture into an ice cream maker and churn according to the manufacturer's instructions. This usually takes about 20-25 minutes, or until the ice cream reaches a soft-serve consistency.
7. **Freeze:**
    1. Transfer the churned ice cream to an airtight container. Freeze for at least 2 hours, or until firm.
8. **Serve:**
    1. Scoop and enjoy your classic strawberry ice cream! For an extra touch, you can garnish with fresh strawberry slices or a sprig of mint.

Relish the refreshing and timeless taste of ripe strawberries in every creamy scoop!

Mango Passionfruit Sorbet

Ingredients:

- 2 cups fresh mango chunks (or frozen, thawed)
- 1 cup passionfruit pulp (fresh or frozen)
- 3/4 cup granulated sugar
- 1/2 cup water
- 1/4 cup freshly squeezed lime juice (about 2 limes)
- 1 teaspoon lime zest (optional, for extra flavor)
- A pinch of salt

Instructions:

1. **Prepare Mango Puree:**
   1. In a blender or food processor, combine the mango chunks and granulated sugar. Blend until smooth.
   2. Add the passionfruit pulp and blend until fully incorporated.
2. **Combine Ingredients:**
   1. In a small bowl, dissolve the sugar in the water by stirring until the sugar is completely dissolved. Add this sugar syrup to the mango-passionfruit mixture.
   2. Stir in the freshly squeezed lime juice and lime zest (if using). Mix well.
3. **Chill Mixture:**
   1. Cover the mixture and refrigerate for at least 1 hour, or until it is thoroughly chilled.
4. **Churn Sorbet:**
   1. Pour the chilled mixture into an ice cream maker and churn according to the manufacturer's instructions. This usually takes about 20-25 minutes, or until the sorbet reaches a smooth, slushy texture.
5. **Freeze:**
   1. Transfer the churned sorbet to an airtight container. Freeze for at least 2 hours, or until firm.
6. **Serve:**
   1. Scoop and enjoy your vibrant and refreshing Mango Passionfruit Sorbet! For an extra touch, garnish with a few fresh mint leaves or a slice of lime.

Delight in the tropical flavors of mango and passionfruit with each refreshing scoop!

Tiramisu Gelato

Ingredients:

For the Gelato Base:

- 2 cups whole milk
- 1 cup heavy cream
- 3/4 cup granulated sugar
- 1/2 cup mascarpone cheese
- 1/4 cup strong brewed coffee, cooled
- 1/4 cup coffee liqueur (optional, for extra depth of flavor)
- 3 large egg yolks
- 1 teaspoon vanilla extract
- A pinch of salt

For the Coffee Swirl:

- 1/4 cup strong brewed coffee (cooled)
- 2 tablespoons granulated sugar
- 1 tablespoon coffee liqueur (optional)

For the Mascarpone Cream:

- 1/2 cup mascarpone cheese
- 2 tablespoons powdered sugar
- 1/2 teaspoon vanilla extract

Instructions:

1. **Prepare Coffee Swirl:**
    1. In a small bowl, combine the cooled coffee, granulated sugar, and coffee liqueur (if using). Stir until the sugar is dissolved. Set aside.
2. **Prepare Gelato Base:**
    1. In a medium saucepan, heat the whole milk and heavy cream over medium heat until it begins to steam but does not boil.
    2. In a separate bowl, whisk together the granulated sugar and egg yolks until pale and smooth.
    3. Gradually whisk the warm milk mixture into the egg yolks to temper them. Return the mixture to the saucepan and cook over medium heat, stirring constantly, until it thickens slightly and coats the back of a spoon (about 5-7 minutes). Do not let it boil.
    4. Remove from heat and stir in the mascarpone cheese, cooled brewed coffee, coffee liqueur (if using), vanilla extract, and a pinch of salt. Mix until smooth and well combined.
3. **Chill Mixture:**
    1. Pour the mixture through a fine-mesh sieve into a clean bowl to remove any lumps.
    2. Cover and refrigerate for at least 1-2 hours, or until thoroughly chilled.

4. **Churn Gelato:**
    1. Pour the chilled mixture into an ice cream maker and churn according to the manufacturer's instructions. This usually takes about 20-25 minutes, or until the gelato reaches a soft-serve consistency.
5. **Prepare Mascarpone Cream:**
    1. In a small bowl, whisk together the mascarpone cheese, powdered sugar, and vanilla extract until smooth and creamy.
6. **Add Swirl and Mascarpone Cream:**
    1. During the last 5 minutes of churning, gently swirl in the prepared coffee swirl mixture and fold in dollops of the mascarpone cream to create a layered effect.
7. **Freeze:**
    1. Transfer the churned gelato to an airtight container. Freeze for at least 2 hours, or until firm.
8. **Serve:**
    1. Scoop and enjoy your luxurious Tiramisu Gelato! For an added touch, you can garnish with a sprinkle of cocoa powder or some finely grated dark chocolate.

Experience the rich and creamy flavors of tiramisu in every spoonful of this decadent gelato!

Fig and Honey Ice Cream

Ingredients:

For the Fig Puree:

- 2 cups fresh figs, stemmed and chopped (or dried figs, soaked and chopped)
- 1/4 cup honey
- 1 tablespoon lemon juice

For the Ice Cream Base:

- 2 cups whole milk
- 1 cup heavy cream
- 3/4 cup granulated sugar
- 1/2 cup honey
- 4 large egg yolks
- 1 teaspoon vanilla extract
- A pinch of salt

Instructions:

1. **Prepare Fig Puree:**
    1. In a medium saucepan, combine the chopped figs, honey, and lemon juice.
    2. Cook over medium heat, stirring occasionally, until the figs are soft and the mixture thickens slightly (about 10-15 minutes).
    3. Allow the mixture to cool slightly, then blend until smooth in a blender or food processor. Set aside.
2. **Prepare Ice Cream Base:**
    1. In a medium saucepan, heat the whole milk and heavy cream over medium heat until it begins to steam but does not boil.
    2. In a separate bowl, whisk together the granulated sugar, honey, and egg yolks until smooth and pale.
    3. Gradually whisk the warm milk mixture into the egg yolks to temper them. Return the mixture to the saucepan and cook over medium heat, stirring constantly, until it thickens slightly and coats the back of a spoon (about 5-7 minutes). Do not let it boil.
    4. Remove from heat and stir in the vanilla extract and a pinch of salt.
3. **Combine Mixtures:**
    1. Allow the custard base to cool to room temperature.
    2. Stir in the fig puree until fully combined.
4. **Chill Mixture:**
    1. Cover and refrigerate for at least 1-2 hours, or until thoroughly chilled.
5. **Churn Ice Cream:**
    1. Pour the chilled mixture into an ice cream maker and churn according to the manufacturer's instructions. This usually takes about 20-25 minutes, or until the ice cream reaches a soft-serve consistency.
6. **Freeze:**

1. Transfer the churned ice cream to an airtight container. Freeze for at least 2 hours, or until firm.
7. **Serve:**
   1. Scoop and enjoy your creamy Fig and Honey Ice Cream! For an extra touch, you can garnish with a drizzle of honey or a few fresh fig slices.

Enjoy the luscious combination of sweet figs and honey in every creamy bite!

Matcha Red Bean Sorbet

Ingredients:

For the Matcha Base:

- 2 cups water
- 1 cup granulated sugar
- 2 tablespoons matcha powder
- 1/2 cup freshly squeezed lemon juice (about 2 lemons)
- 1/2 teaspoon vanilla extract
- A pinch of salt

For the Red Bean Swirl:

- 1 cup sweetened red bean paste (anko, store-bought or homemade)
- 2 tablespoons water (to loosen the paste)

Instructions:

1. **Prepare Matcha Mixture:**
   1. In a medium saucepan, heat 1 cup of water and the granulated sugar over medium heat, stirring until the sugar is completely dissolved.
   2. In a bowl, whisk together the matcha powder with the remaining 1 cup of cold water until smooth and fully dissolved.
   3. Add the matcha mixture to the sugar syrup in the saucepan and stir to combine.
   4. Remove from heat and stir in the freshly squeezed lemon juice, vanilla extract, and a pinch of salt. Mix well.
2. **Chill Mixture:**
   1. Allow the matcha mixture to cool to room temperature, then cover and refrigerate for at least 1-2 hours, or until thoroughly chilled.
3. **Prepare Red Bean Swirl:**
   1. In a small bowl, mix the sweetened red bean paste with 2 tablespoons of water to loosen it slightly. You want it to be spreadable but not too runny.
4. **Churn Sorbet:**
   1. Pour the chilled matcha mixture into an ice cream maker and churn according to the manufacturer's instructions. This usually takes about 20-25 minutes, or until the sorbet reaches a soft-serve consistency.
5. **Add Red Bean Swirl:**
   1. During the last 5 minutes of churning, gently fold in dollops of the red bean paste to create a swirl effect.
6. **Freeze:**
   1. Transfer the churned sorbet to an airtight container. Freeze for at least 2 hours, or until firm.
7. **Serve:**
   1. Scoop and enjoy your refreshing Matcha Red Bean Sorbet! For an extra touch, garnish with a sprinkle of matcha powder or a few red bean pieces.

Savor the harmonious blend of earthy matcha and sweet red beans in this unique and refreshing sorbet!

S'mores Frozen Custard

Ingredients:

For the Custard Base:

- 2 cups whole milk
- 1 cup heavy cream
- 3/4 cup granulated sugar
- 4 large egg yolks
- 1/2 teaspoon vanilla extract
- A pinch of salt

For the S'mores Mix-Ins:

- 1 cup graham cracker crumbs
- 1 cup mini marshmallows
- 1/2 cup chocolate chips (semi-sweet or milk chocolate)

Instructions:

1. **Prepare Custard Base:**
    1. In a medium saucepan, heat the whole milk and heavy cream over medium heat until it begins to steam but does not boil.
    2. In a separate bowl, whisk together the granulated sugar and egg yolks until smooth and pale.
    3. Gradually whisk the warm milk mixture into the egg yolks to temper them. Return the mixture to the saucepan and cook over medium heat, stirring constantly, until it thickens slightly and coats the back of a spoon (about 5-7 minutes). Do not let it boil.
    4. Remove from heat and stir in the vanilla extract and a pinch of salt.
2. **Chill Mixture:**
    1. Pour the custard base through a fine-mesh sieve into a clean bowl to remove any lumps.
    2. Cover and refrigerate for at least 1-2 hours, or until thoroughly chilled.
3. **Churn Custard:**
    1. Pour the chilled custard base into an ice cream maker and churn according to the manufacturer's instructions. This usually takes about 20-25 minutes, or until the custard reaches a soft-serve consistency.
4. **Add S'mores Mix-Ins:**
    1. During the last 5 minutes of churning, gently fold in the graham cracker crumbs, mini marshmallows, and chocolate chips to evenly distribute them throughout the custard.
5. **Freeze:**
    1. Transfer the churned custard to an airtight container. Freeze for at least 2 hours, or until firm.
6. **Serve:**

1. Scoop and enjoy your indulgent S'mores Frozen Custard! For an extra touch, you can garnish with additional graham cracker crumbs, mini marshmallows, or a drizzle of chocolate sauce.

Enjoy the delicious combination of creamy custard with classic s'mores flavors in every spoonful!

Pineapple Mint Gelato

Ingredients:

For the Pineapple Mixture:

- 2 cups fresh pineapple chunks (or frozen, thawed)
- 1/2 cup granulated sugar
- 1 tablespoon freshly squeezed lime juice (about 1 lime)
- 1 teaspoon lime zest (optional, for extra flavor)

For the Gelato Base:

- 2 cups whole milk
- 1 cup heavy cream
- 3/4 cup granulated sugar
- 1/2 cup finely chopped fresh mint leaves (or 2 teaspoons dried mint)
- 1 teaspoon vanilla extract
- A pinch of salt

Instructions:

1. **Prepare Pineapple Puree:**
    1. In a blender or food processor, blend the pineapple chunks with 1/2 cup of granulated sugar until smooth.
    2. Stir in the freshly squeezed lime juice and lime zest (if using). Set aside.
2. **Infuse Milk with Mint:**
    1. In a medium saucepan, heat the whole milk and 1 cup of heavy cream over medium heat until it begins to steam but does not boil.
    2. Add the finely chopped fresh mint leaves (or dried mint) and let it steep in the warm milk mixture for about 5 minutes, stirring occasionally.
    3. Strain the mint leaves out of the milk mixture using a fine-mesh sieve.
3. **Prepare Gelato Base:**
    1. In a large bowl, whisk together 3/4 cup granulated sugar and a pinch of salt.
    2. Gradually whisk the warm milk mixture into the sugar until fully dissolved and combined.
    3. Stir in the vanilla extract.
4. **Combine Mixtures:**
    1. Allow the milk mixture to cool to room temperature.
    2. Stir in the pineapple puree until well combined.
5. **Chill Mixture:**
    1. Cover and refrigerate the mixture for at least 1-2 hours, or until it is thoroughly chilled.
6. **Churn Gelato:**
    1. Pour the chilled mixture into an ice cream maker and churn according to the manufacturer's instructions. This usually takes about 20-25 minutes, or until the gelato reaches a soft-serve consistency.
7. **Freeze:**

1. Transfer the churned gelato to an airtight container. Freeze for at least 2 hours, or until firm.
8. **Serve:**
   1. Scoop and enjoy your refreshing Pineapple Mint Gelato! For an extra touch, you can garnish with a sprig of fresh mint or a few pineapple chunks.

Delight in the tropical fusion of pineapple and mint with each creamy, refreshing scoop!

Chai Tea Ice Cream

Ingredients:

For the Chai Tea Base:

- 2 cups whole milk
- 1 cup heavy cream
- 3/4 cup granulated sugar
- 4-5 chai tea bags (or 3-4 tablespoons loose-leaf chai tea)
- 4 large egg yolks
- 1 teaspoon vanilla extract
- A pinch of salt

For the Chai Spice Mix (optional, for extra flavor):

- 1/2 teaspoon ground cinnamon
- 1/4 teaspoon ground cardamom
- 1/4 teaspoon ground ginger
- 1/8 teaspoon ground cloves

Instructions:

1. **Infuse Milk with Chai Tea:**
    1. In a medium saucepan, heat the whole milk and heavy cream over medium heat until it begins to steam but does not boil.
    2. Remove from heat and add the chai tea bags or loose-leaf tea (using a tea infuser). Steep for 5-7 minutes, depending on how strong you want the chai flavor to be. Remove the tea bags or strain out the loose tea.
2. **Prepare Custard Base:**
    1. In a separate bowl, whisk together the granulated sugar and egg yolks until smooth and pale.
    2. Gradually whisk the warm milk mixture into the egg yolks to temper them.
    3. Return the mixture to the saucepan and cook over medium heat, stirring constantly, until it thickens slightly and coats the back of a spoon (about 5-7 minutes). Do not let it boil.
    4. Remove from heat and stir in the vanilla extract, a pinch of salt, and the optional chai spice mix if using.
3. **Chill Mixture:**
    1. Pour the custard base through a fine-mesh sieve into a clean bowl to remove any lumps.
    2. Allow the mixture to cool to room temperature.
    3. Cover and refrigerate for at least 1-2 hours, or until thoroughly chilled.
4. **Churn Ice Cream:**
    1. Pour the chilled mixture into an ice cream maker and churn according to the manufacturer's instructions. This usually takes about 20-25 minutes, or until the ice cream reaches a soft-serve consistency.
5. **Freeze:**

        1. Transfer the churned ice cream to an airtight container. Freeze for at least 2 hours, or until firm.
    6. **Serve:**
        1. Scoop and enjoy your flavorful Chai Tea Ice Cream! For an extra touch, you can garnish with a sprinkle of cinnamon or a cinnamon stick.

Indulge in the aromatic spices of chai tea blended perfectly into a creamy, dreamy ice cream!

Pear Vanilla Sorbet

Ingredients:

- 4 ripe pears, peeled, cored, and chopped
- 3/4 cup granulated sugar
- 1/2 cup water
- 1 tablespoon freshly squeezed lemon juice (about 1 lemon)
- 1 teaspoon vanilla extract
- A pinch of salt

Instructions:

1. **Prepare Pear Puree:**
    1. In a blender or food processor, blend the chopped pears until smooth.
    2. In a small saucepan, combine the water and granulated sugar. Heat over medium heat, stirring until the sugar is completely dissolved. Allow to cool.
2. **Combine Ingredients:**
    1. Stir the cooled sugar syrup into the pear puree.
    2. Add the freshly squeezed lemon juice, vanilla extract, and a pinch of salt. Mix well.
3. **Chill Mixture:**
    1. Cover the mixture and refrigerate for at least 1-2 hours, or until thoroughly chilled.
4. **Churn Sorbet:**
    1. Pour the chilled mixture into an ice cream maker and churn according to the manufacturer's instructions. This usually takes about 20-25 minutes, or until the sorbet reaches a smooth, slushy texture.
5. **Freeze:**
    1. Transfer the churned sorbet to an airtight container. Freeze for at least 2 hours, or until firm.
6. **Serve:**
    1. Scoop and enjoy your refreshing Pear Vanilla Sorbet! For an extra touch, you can garnish with a few fresh mint leaves or a thin slice of pear.

Savor the delicate flavor of ripe pears enhanced by vanilla in every refreshing scoop!

Dark Chocolate Chili Ice Cream

Ingredients:

For the Ice Cream Base:

- 2 cups whole milk
- 1 cup heavy cream
- 3/4 cup granulated sugar
- 1/2 cup unsweetened cocoa powder
- 4 large egg yolks
- 4 oz dark chocolate (70% cocoa), chopped
- 1 teaspoon vanilla extract
- A pinch of salt

For the Chili Spice Mix:

- 1/2 teaspoon ground chili powder
- 1/4 teaspoon ground cayenne pepper (adjust to taste)
- 1/4 teaspoon ground cinnamon

Instructions:

1. **Prepare Chocolate Base:**
    1. In a medium saucepan, heat the whole milk and heavy cream over medium heat until it begins to steam but does not boil.
    2. In a separate bowl, whisk together the granulated sugar and cocoa powder until well combined.
    3. Gradually whisk the warm milk mixture into the sugar and cocoa powder until smooth and fully combined.
    4. Return the mixture to the saucepan and cook over medium heat, stirring constantly, until it thickens slightly and coats the back of a spoon (about 5-7 minutes). Do not let it boil.
2. **Combine Egg Yolks:**
    1. In a separate bowl, whisk the egg yolks until smooth.
    2. Gradually whisk a small amount of the hot chocolate mixture into the egg yolks to temper them.
    3. Return the egg yolk mixture to the saucepan and cook, stirring constantly, until it thickens slightly and coats the back of a spoon (about 2-3 minutes). Do not let it boil.
3. **Add Chocolate and Flavorings:**
    1. Remove from heat and stir in the chopped dark chocolate until melted and smooth.
    2. Add the vanilla extract, a pinch of salt, and the chili spice mix (chili powder, cayenne pepper, and cinnamon). Mix well.
4. **Chill Mixture:**
    1. Pour the mixture through a fine-mesh sieve into a clean bowl to remove any lumps.
    2. Allow the custard base to cool to room temperature.

       3. Cover and refrigerate for at least 1-2 hours, or until thoroughly chilled.
5. **Churn Ice Cream:**
    1. Pour the chilled mixture into an ice cream maker and churn according to the manufacturer's instructions. This usually takes about 20-25 minutes, or until the ice cream reaches a soft-serve consistency.
6. **Freeze:**
    1. Transfer the churned ice cream to an airtight container. Freeze for at least 2 hours, or until firm.
7. **Serve:**
    1. Scoop and enjoy your bold and spicy Dark Chocolate Chili Ice Cream! For an extra touch, you can garnish with a sprinkle of chili powder or a few shavings of dark chocolate.

Experience the thrilling combination of rich dark chocolate and spicy chili in each adventurous scoop!

Coconut Lychee Gelato

Ingredients:

For the Coconut Mixture:

- 1 can (14 oz) full-fat coconut milk
- 1 cup heavy cream
- 1/2 cup granulated sugar
- 1/2 cup shredded coconut (unsweetened or sweetened, based on preference)
- 1 teaspoon vanilla extract
- A pinch of salt

For the Lychee Puree:

- 1 can (20 oz) lychee fruit in syrup (or fresh lychees, peeled and pitted)
- 1/4 cup granulated sugar (adjust based on sweetness of lychees)
- 1 tablespoon freshly squeezed lime juice (about 1 lime)

Instructions:

1. **Prepare Lychee Puree:**
    1. Drain the lychees, reserving a few for garnish if desired.
    2. In a blender or food processor, blend the lychees until smooth.
    3. Add the granulated sugar and lime juice. Blend again until well combined. Adjust sweetness as needed.
2. **Prepare Coconut Mixture:**
    1. In a medium saucepan, heat the coconut milk and heavy cream over medium heat until it begins to steam but does not boil.
    2. Stir in the granulated sugar and shredded coconut. Cook, stirring occasionally, until the sugar is dissolved and the mixture is well combined.
    3. Remove from heat and stir in the vanilla extract and a pinch of salt.
3. **Combine Mixtures:**
    1. Allow the coconut mixture to cool to room temperature.
    2. Once cooled, stir in the lychee puree until fully combined.
4. **Chill Mixture:**
    1. Cover the mixture and refrigerate for at least 1-2 hours, or until thoroughly chilled.
5. **Churn Gelato:**
    1. Pour the chilled mixture into an ice cream maker and churn according to the manufacturer's instructions. This usually takes about 20-25 minutes, or until the gelato reaches a soft-serve consistency.
6. **Freeze:**
    1. Transfer the churned gelato to an airtight container. Freeze for at least 2 hours, or until firm.
7. **Serve:**
    1. Scoop and enjoy your creamy Coconut Lychee Gelato! For an extra touch, you can garnish with a few fresh lychee pieces or a sprinkle of toasted coconut.

Delight in the exotic blend of creamy coconut and sweet, floral lychee in every refreshing scoop!

Blackberry Lemonade Granita

Ingredients:

- 2 cups fresh blackberries (or frozen, thawed)
- 1 cup granulated sugar
- 1 cup freshly squeezed lemon juice (about 4-6 lemons)
- 1 cup water
- 1 tablespoon lemon zest (optional, for extra citrus flavor)
- A pinch of salt

Instructions:

1. **Prepare Blackberry Puree:**
    1. In a blender or food processor, blend the blackberries until smooth.
    2. Strain the blackberry puree through a fine-mesh sieve into a bowl to remove the seeds.
2. **Prepare Lemonade Mixture:**
    1. In a medium bowl, whisk together the granulated sugar and water until the sugar is completely dissolved.
    2. Stir in the freshly squeezed lemon juice and lemon zest (if using).
    3. Add a pinch of salt to balance the flavors.
3. **Combine Mixtures:**
    1. Stir the blackberry puree into the lemonade mixture until well combined.
4. **Freeze:**
    1. Pour the mixture into a shallow baking dish or pan.
    2. Place in the freezer and freeze for about 2 hours, or until the edges start to freeze.
5. **Scrape Granita:**
    1. Use a fork to scrape and stir the mixture every 30 minutes to break up any ice crystals and create a flaky texture. Continue scraping until the entire mixture has a granular, fluffy texture (about 4-5 hours).
6. **Serve:**
    1. Scoop the granita into glasses or bowls.
    2. Garnish with fresh blackberries or a mint sprig, if desired.

Enjoy the refreshing and tangy combination of blackberries and lemonade in this easy, icy treat!

Brownie Batter Frozen Yogurt

Ingredients:

For the Frozen Yogurt Base:

- 2 cups plain Greek yogurt (full-fat or 2%)
- 1 cup heavy cream
- 1/2 cup granulated sugar
- 1/2 cup brown sugar
- 1 teaspoon vanilla extract
- A pinch of salt

For the Brownie Batter Swirl:

- 1/2 cup brownie mix (dry)
- 2 tablespoons unsweetened cocoa powder
- 1/4 cup milk (whole or 2%)
- 1/4 cup butter, melted
- 1/4 cup mini chocolate chips (optional, for extra texture)

Instructions:

1. **Prepare Frozen Yogurt Base:**
    1. In a large bowl, whisk together the plain Greek yogurt, heavy cream, granulated sugar, brown sugar, vanilla extract, and a pinch of salt until smooth and the sugars are fully dissolved.
2. **Prepare Brownie Batter Swirl:**
    1. In a small bowl, combine the brownie mix and unsweetened cocoa powder.
    2. Gradually add the milk and melted butter, stirring until smooth and combined. You want a thick but spreadable consistency.
    3. If using, stir in the mini chocolate chips.
3. **Churn Frozen Yogurt:**
    1. Pour the yogurt mixture into an ice cream maker and churn according to the manufacturer's instructions. This usually takes about 20-25 minutes, or until the yogurt reaches a soft-serve consistency.
4. **Add Brownie Batter Swirl:**
    1. During the last 5 minutes of churning, spoon dollops of the brownie batter into the churned yogurt. Gently fold in the brownie batter to create a swirl effect. Be careful not to over-mix; you want distinct swirls of brownie batter.
5. **Freeze:**
    1. Transfer the frozen yogurt to an airtight container. Freeze for at least 2 hours, or until firm.
6. **Serve:**
    1. Scoop and enjoy your indulgent Brownie Batter Frozen Yogurt! For an extra treat, you can top with additional mini chocolate chips or a drizzle of chocolate sauce.

Enjoy the rich, fudgy brownie batter blended with creamy frozen yogurt in every delicious bite!

Pomegranate Citrus Sorbet

Ingredients:

- 2 cups pomegranate juice (freshly squeezed or store-bought)
- 1 cup freshly squeezed orange juice (about 2-3 oranges)

- 1/2 cup freshly squeezed lemon juice (about 2 lemons)
- 3/4 cup granulated sugar (adjust to taste)
- 1/2 cup water
- 1 tablespoon orange zest (optional, for extra citrus flavor)
- 1 tablespoon lemon zest (optional, for extra citrus flavor)
- A pinch of salt

Instructions:

1. **Prepare Syrup:**
    1. In a small saucepan, combine the water and granulated sugar. Heat over medium heat, stirring occasionally, until the sugar is completely dissolved. Allow the syrup to cool.
2. **Combine Juices:**
    1. In a large bowl, mix together the pomegranate juice, orange juice, and lemon juice.
    2. Stir in the cooled syrup and a pinch of salt. Adjust sweetness to taste. If using, add the orange and lemon zest for extra flavor.
3. **Chill Mixture:**
    1. Cover the mixture and refrigerate for at least 1-2 hours, or until thoroughly chilled.
4. **Freeze Sorbet:**
    1. Pour the chilled mixture into an ice cream maker and churn according to the manufacturer's instructions. This usually takes about 20-25 minutes, or until the sorbet reaches a slushy, soft-serve consistency.
5. **Freeze:**
    1. Transfer the churned sorbet to an airtight container. Freeze for at least 2 hours, or until firm.
6. **Serve:**
    1. Scoop and enjoy your refreshing Pomegranate Citrus Sorbet! For an extra touch, garnish with a few pomegranate seeds or a sprig of mint.

Experience the bright, tangy combination of pomegranate and citrus in this refreshing and vibrant sorbet!

Spumoni Ice Cream

Ingredients:

For the Cherry Layer:

- 1 cup sweetened cherry puree (fresh or jarred)
- 1 cup heavy cream
- 1/2 cup whole milk
- 1/2 cup granulated sugar
- 1/2 teaspoon vanilla extract

For the Pistachio Layer:

- 1 cup shelled pistachios, finely ground
- 1 cup heavy cream
- 1/2 cup whole milk
- 1/2 cup granulated sugar
- 1/4 teaspoon almond extract
- A pinch of salt

For the Chocolate Layer:

- 1 cup heavy cream
- 1/2 cup whole milk
- 1/2 cup granulated sugar
- 1/2 cup unsweetened cocoa powder
- 1/2 cup semi-sweet chocolate chips, chopped
- 1/2 teaspoon vanilla extract

Instructions:

1. **Prepare Cherry Layer:**
    1. In a bowl, whisk together the cherry puree, 1 cup heavy cream, 1/2 cup whole milk, granulated sugar, and vanilla extract until the sugar is dissolved.
    2. Pour the mixture into an ice cream maker and churn according to the manufacturer's instructions. This usually takes about 20-25 minutes, or until it reaches a soft-serve consistency.
2. **Prepare Pistachio Layer:**
    1. In a bowl, whisk together the finely ground pistachios, 1 cup heavy cream, 1/2 cup whole milk, granulated sugar, almond extract, and a pinch of salt until the sugar is dissolved.
    2. Pour the mixture into the ice cream maker and churn according to the manufacturer's instructions. This usually takes about 20-25 minutes, or until it reaches a soft-serve consistency.
3. **Prepare Chocolate Layer:**
    1. In a saucepan, heat 1 cup heavy cream and 1/2 cup whole milk over medium heat until it begins to steam but does not boil.
    2. In a bowl, whisk together the granulated sugar and unsweetened cocoa powder.
    3. Gradually whisk the warm cream mixture into the cocoa mixture until smooth.

       4. Stir in the chopped chocolate chips and heat gently until fully melted and combined.
       5. Remove from heat and stir in the vanilla extract. Allow to cool to room temperature.
4. **Layer and Freeze:**
       1. Transfer the churned cherry ice cream to an airtight container and smooth the top.
       2. Spread the churned pistachio ice cream over the cherry layer.
       3. Finally, pour the chocolate mixture over the pistachio layer.
       4. Use a spatula to swirl the layers slightly for a marbled effect, if desired.
5. **Freeze:**
       1. Cover and freeze the assembled spumoni for at least 2 hours, or until firm.
6. **Serve:**
       1. Scoop and enjoy your classic Spumoni Ice Cream! For an extra touch, you can garnish with a few chopped pistachios or a cherry.

Delight in the harmonious blend of cherry, pistachio, and chocolate in this traditional Italian dessert!

Banana Cream Pie Gelato

Ingredients:

For the Banana Base:

- 2 ripe bananas, mashed
- 1 cup whole milk
- 1 cup heavy cream
- 3/4 cup granulated sugar
- 1/2 teaspoon vanilla extract
- 1/2 teaspoon lemon juice
- A pinch of salt

For the Pie Crust Swirl:

- 1/2 cup graham cracker crumbs
- 2 tablespoons granulated sugar
- 2 tablespoons unsalted butter, melted

For the Vanilla Custard Layer:

- 1 cup whole milk
- 1/2 cup heavy cream
- 1/4 cup granulated sugar
- 2 large egg yolks
- 1/2 teaspoon vanilla extract

Instructions:

1. **Prepare Banana Base:**
    1. In a medium bowl, whisk together the mashed bananas, whole milk, heavy cream, granulated sugar, vanilla extract, lemon juice, and a pinch of salt until smooth and the sugar is fully dissolved.
    2. Cover and refrigerate the banana mixture for at least 1-2 hours, or until thoroughly chilled.
2. **Prepare Vanilla Custard Layer:**
    1. In a medium saucepan, heat 1 cup whole milk and 1/2 cup heavy cream over medium heat until it begins to steam but does not boil.
    2. In a separate bowl, whisk together 1/4 cup granulated sugar and 2 large egg yolks until smooth.
    3. Gradually whisk the warm milk mixture into the egg yolks to temper them. Return the mixture to the saucepan and cook over medium heat, stirring constantly, until it thickens slightly and coats the back of a spoon (about 5-7 minutes). Do not let it boil.
    4. Remove from heat and stir in 1/2 teaspoon vanilla extract.
    5. Allow the custard to cool to room temperature, then cover and refrigerate until chilled.
3. **Prepare Pie Crust Swirl:**

    1. In a small bowl, mix together the graham cracker crumbs, granulated sugar, and melted butter until well combined and crumbly.
4. **Churn Banana Gelato:**
    1. Pour the chilled banana mixture into an ice cream maker and churn according to the manufacturer's instructions. This usually takes about 20-25 minutes, or until it reaches a soft-serve consistency.
5. **Combine Layers:**
    1. Transfer half of the churned banana gelato to an airtight container.
    2. Gently swirl in half of the vanilla custard layer and a handful of the graham cracker crumb mixture.
    3. Add the remaining banana gelato on top, then swirl in the remaining vanilla custard layer and graham cracker crumbs.
6. **Freeze:**
    1. Cover and freeze the assembled gelato for at least 2 hours, or until firm.
7. **Serve:**
    1. Scoop and enjoy your delicious Banana Cream Pie Gelato! For an extra touch, garnish with additional graham cracker crumbs or a slice of fresh banana.

Enjoy the rich flavors of banana cream pie with every creamy, indulgent scoop!

www.ingramcontent.com/pod-product-compliance
Lightning Source LLC
LaVergne TN
LVHW061947070526
838199LV00060B/4018